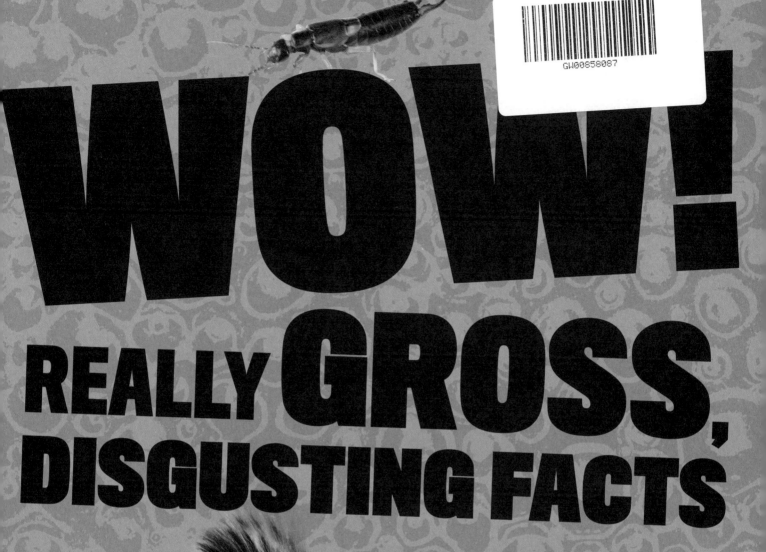

WOW!
REALLY GROSS, DISGUSTING FACTS

GW00858087

This edition published by Parragon Books Ltd in 2016

Parragon Books Ltd
Chartist House
15–17 Trim Street
Bath BA1 1HA, UK
www.parragon.com

Copyright © Parragon Books Ltd 2014-2016

All rights reserved. No part of this publication may be reproduced, stored in a retrieval system or transmitted, in any form or by any means, electronic, mechanical, photocopying, recording or otherwise, without the prior permission of the copyright holder.

ISBN 978-1-4748-5063-6

Printed in China

WOW!
REALLY GROSS, DISGUSTING FACTS

PaRragon

Bath · New York · Cologne · Melbourne · Delhi
Hong Kong · Shenzhen · Singapore

11 facts about SLIMY SNOT

The scientific word for nose-picking is

RHINOTILLEXOMANIA.

#001

A person **swallows about a litre of snot** a day without even realizing it.

#002

Snot is made of **water, salt and a gluey, sugary substance called mucin...**

#003

... When the water dries out it turns into **hard bogies.**

#004

Snot moves through your breathing tubes at **1.5 centimetres per hour.** Bamboo grass grows more quickly than this.

#005

A sneeze hurtles out snot at over 60 KILOMETRES PER HOUR – that's nearly twice as fast as a London tube train. #006

The world sneezing record is held by British girl Donna Griffiths. She **SNEEZED A MILLION TIMES IN A ROW.** #007

If you've been hanging out in a **dusty room,** your snot will be a **GREY dust-colour.** #008

Your snot looks more **yellow** when you have **a cold** because of all the **white blood cells** in it. #009

YOUR SNOT protects you from dirt and germs in the air by catching them. #010

Snot is more than just sticky goo. It contains **antibodies** that help the body recognize **invading bacteria and viruses,** and creates **enzymes** to help kill them. #011

9 SLOBBERY SPIT FACTS

Your mouth produces between ONE AND TWO LITRES OF SPIT (also known as saliva) a day.

#001

In some parts of the world, it is thought that a **mother's saliva can help build up a child's immune system,** so mums chew their baby's food before feeding it to them.

#002

Your saliva turns your food into a SOUP-LIKE MIXTURE, which makes it easier to swallow.

#003

Yawning really hard can make your spit spray **more than a metre.** This is called **GLEEKING.**

#004

In Singapore, you can be fined £1300 for spitting in the street.

#005

A single COW

makes as much saliva as **200 HUMANS.** It helps them to chew all that grass. #006

FULMAR CHICKS SPIT

at other animals to keep them away. #007

Llamas spit when they get annoyed. Their spit is super-smelly because it includes food from their stomach. #008

Spitting cobras spit painful venom **straight into the eyes of predators,** and then slither away to safety. #009

3 VILE VOMIT FACTS

Vomit is very **ACIDIC** and **dissolves your teeth.** #001

Vomit contains half-digested food and bits of stomach lining, which look like **lumps of carrot.** #002

When one person vomits, it makes **everyone** around them feel sick, too. This can be useful if you've all eaten something **poisonous.** #003

5 PONGY POO FACTS

Your poo smells because of stinky chemicals called **skatole** and **indole.**

#001

People fart 14 times a day.

#002

Cabbage contains **stinky sulphur,** which gives you **smelly farts.**

#003

1/3 of your **poo** is made of bacteria.

#004

Sweetcorn passes straight through you, and comes out looking **EXACTLY THE SAME** as when it went in. This is because you cannot digest its tough, fibrous kernels.

#005

11 facts about PEE

When it first comes out, pee is **cleaner** than spit. #001

urine is **95** percent **water.** #002

The other **5 per cent** is old body cells, unwanted material from your food and salt. #003

Ancient Egyptian doctors used to taste people's urine to find out if they were diabetic. #004

You pee between one and two litres of urine a day. #005

Some people think **drinking your own pee** makes you healthier. #006

Throughout your life, you pee about 45,000 litres of urine. #007

That's enough to fill a small swimming pool.

Your pee is yellow because of a chemical called urochrome. #008

You can pee faster or slower by controlling the muscles underneath your bladder. #009

Male lobsters have bladders in their heads, and shoot pee at each other. #010

If you eat **asparagus**, your pee will smell of it. #011

5 Facts about Burping

Swallowing air as you eat and drink can make you **BURP and fart.** #001

Burping gets rid of a litre of gas from your **stomach** every day. #002

Drinking through a straw can **make you burp,** because you swallow more air. #003

In the zero gravity of space, **ASTRONAUTS WET BURP** because some of their stomach contents come out, too. #004

The **LOUDEST BURP** ever recorded was as loud as a **car alarm.** #005

50 yucky food facts

The gelling agent used in most jellies is gelatin and is sourced from animals. #001 You can buy cow tongue ice cream in Tokyo. #002 Carmine is a red food colouring that comes from boiled cochineal beetle – it is used in sweets. #003 Honey is made from nectar and bee vomit. #004 An edible snail is called an escargot. #005 Snails have been eaten since Roman times. #006 Haggis is made from the heart, lungs, liver and kidneys of a sheep. #007 Garum, a fish sauce, was the Ancient Greeks' and Romans' favourite condiment. #008 It was made from rotten fish. #009 More than 1900 species of insect are eaten around the world. #010 Fried locusts are a Nigerian delicacy. #011 They taste a little like prawns. #012 In Cambodia, large spiders fried with garlic are a popular dish. #013 American Indians roast beetles and munch on them like popcorn. #014 People in Bali catch dragonflies with a stick coated in sticky plant juice. #015 They then fry them and eat them. #016 Japanese athletes drink giant hornet juice. #017 Food markets in Beijing in China offer candied scorpions on a stick. #018 In Laos, people eat red ants tossed with salad. #019 In 2013 a group of London students opened a restaurant specializing in insects. #020 Dishes included watermelon with caterpillar risotto and ground-up cricket. #021 Roman Emperor Nero started eating dinner in the afternoon. #022 He would finish eating around dawn! #023 Sumo wrestlers eat two giant pots of meat stew every day. #024 This is to make sure they're heavy enough to fight. #025 Over 2 billion people around the world are overweight. #026 About 805 million people around the world are ill with malnutrition. #027 A lack of vitamin B can cause hair loss and tiredness. #028 A type of Sardinian cheese has maggots put in it on purpose. #029 Cider makers used to add meat to their mixture of apples and water. As the meat rotted, it helped the mixture turn to cider. #030 The meat was usually livestock, but sometimes it came from the rats that fell into the mixture by accident. #031 Salami develops a mould around its casing while it's being made. #032 The mould is left on to give it more flavour. #033 Some wine makers use mouldy grapes to make sweet wines. #034 Kopi Luwak is the world's most expensive coffee. #035 It's made from beans eaten then pooed out by a small animal called a palm civet. #036 Kiviak is an Inuit meal made by stuffing 500 birds into the body of a seal. #037 This is then eaten by making a hole in the neck and sucking out the juices. #038 White truffles are edible fungi that sell for thousands of pounds per kilogram. #039 Miso is a Japanese paste made from rice, barley and soybeans. #040 This mixture is then combined with fungus. #041 In China, it's considered a delicacy to leave eggs to rot for months, turning their yolks green, before they're eaten. #042 A Limburger sandwich is filled with raw onion, mustard and Limburger cheese, which smells like body odour. #043 Offal is the internal organs of an animal. #044 The rubbery lining of a cow's stomach is called tripe. #045 Black pudding is a blood sausage cooked until it goes solid. #046 Head cheese is the meat from a pig's head, set in jelly. #047 Ox brain fritters are popular in Cuba. #048 Thrips are tiny insects that hide in fruit and vegetables. #049 Oregano can legally contain up to 1250 insect fragments per 10 g. #050

5 FOOD-EATING RECORD facts

The largest number of **oysters swallowed in 3 minutes** is **233.**

#001

In 2006, Japanese eating champion Takeru Kobayashi ate **97 HAMBURGERS** in **10 minutes,** beating his own world record by 28.

#002

Every day, Americans consume about 20 million hamburgers and 9 million pizzas.

#003

American Joey Chestnut is a world champion competitive eater. **In 2013, he beat his own record by scoffing 69 HOT DOGS IN 10 MINUTES.**

#004

American Don Lerman ate **seven 100 g sticks of salted butter** in 5 minutes.

#005

8 BAD BACTERIA FACTS

Lots of bacteria live in your armpits and feet. They live off the sweat. #001

A single gram of fluid in your large intestine contains 10 trillion bacteria. #002

There are about 3000 microbes (tiny bacteria) on every square centimetre of a desk. #003

If you could get bacteria to line up in a row, 10,000 would fit across your fingernail. #004

A piece of chicken that is starting to smell is covered with at least 10 million bacteria per square centimetre. #005

Hot water is much better than cold water at getting rid of bacteria from your hands. Most bacteria are frazzled by the heat. #006

A kitchen sink is home to 10,000 times more germs than a toilet. #007

One bacterium can turn into millions of bacteria in less than a day. #008

6 DEADLY DISEASE FACTS

The Black Death killed more than 25 million people across Europe, which was one-third of the population at the time.
#001

More than 220 million people around the world suffer from malaria each year.
#002

The plague germ was spread by rat fleas. It was called Yersinia pestis.
#003

On average, one person catches tuberculosis every 3.6 seconds.
#004

There can be as many as 5 billion viruses in one drop of blood.
#005

Smallpox killed 30 per cent of the people who caught it.
#006

12 FACTS ABOUT PESKY PARASITES

The **average human** body carries between **1 and 2.5 kg** of parasitic bacteria (organisms that feed on a larger host). #001

The largest parasitic worm ever found

was **8.5 m** long. It was found living in a female sperm whale's womb. #002

A tapeworm **can live inside a human gut** for up to 20 years. #003

Tiny **white pinworms** live in your gut, but move to your **BOTTOM** to lay eggs. #004

Parasitic worm eggs get into soil through animal droppings... #005

… There can be **THOUSANDS** of parasitic worm eggs **in one handful of soil**. #006

Flukes are parasitic worms found in **FISH, CATTLE AND SHEEP.** Humans can also become infected by swimming in fluke-infested water. #008

Hookworms can live in your intestine, sucking on **YOUR BLOOD.** #007

Humans can become infected with the parasite *Toxoplasma gondii* by eating undercooked meat, or coming into contact with **infected cat poo**. #009

Thorny-headed worms hatch inside pond crustaceans, which are then eaten by ducks. The worm reproduces inside the duck, and its **eggs come out in the duck's poo.** They are then eaten by a crustacean, and the cycle begins again. #010

A female flea sucks up to **15 TIMES** her own body weight in blood every day.

#011

The **tongue-eating** louse **EATS THE TONGUE** of its fish victim, and lives in its place. #012

19

10 SPIDER FACTS

The female black widow often eats the male after mating.
#001

Poisonous black widows have been found **hiding in bunches of grapes**.
#002

To invade high ground, small spiders can release several threads, which form a **PARACHUTE**. Spiders have been seen as high up as 3000 m.
#003

The venomous redback spider of Australia has been known to **lurk beneath toilet seats**.
#004

Ogre-faced spiders weave a web between their front legs. They use the web like a net to catch any prey that flies into it.
#005

The **biggest spider in the world** is the Goliath bird-eating spider, which is as big as a dinner plate.
#006

Spitting spiders spit a mixture of venom and glue at a victim. This sticks the prey in one place and kills it.
#007

Venomous **Brazilian wandering spiders** can grow up to 13 cm wide, and have been found hidden in bunches of bananas.
#008

The venom of the brown recluse spider is necrotic, meaning that it **rots your flesh**.
#009

Spiders can't digest anything solid. They dissolve food by **injecting digestive juices into their prey**, then they suck up the gloop left behind.
#010

21

9 POISON AND VENOM facts

The land snake with the **most lethal venom** is the **Australian inland taipan.** #001

The **most potent snake venom** of all comes from a Pacific sea snake, but it is peaceful, and won't attack unless very scared. #002

In India, **46,000** people die from snake bites a year – that's more than anywhere else in the world. #003

Some snake venoms work by shutting down the victim's body so that it is still alive but cannot move. #004

The **deadly puffer fish** is a delicacy in Japan, and chefs have to take great care to remove the poison. Even so, about 12 people die each year from eating this fish. #005

The **golden poison frog** has enough deadly poison in it to kill **10 to 20** people. #006

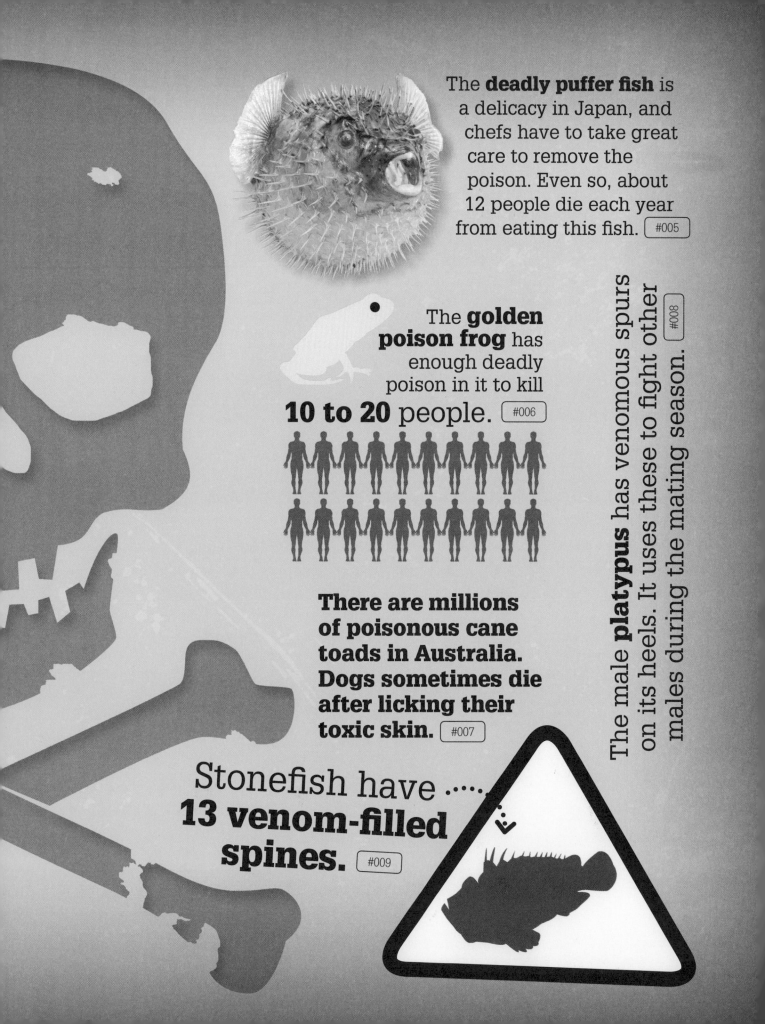

There are millions of poisonous cane toads in Australia. Dogs sometimes die after licking their toxic skin. #007

The male **platypus** has venomous spurs on its heels. It uses these to fight other males during the mating season. #008

Stonefish have ..... **13 venom-filled spines.** #009

100 FACTS
that will make your
SKIN CRAWL

Cockroaches can live for weeks without their heads. [#001] There are about 4000 different species of cockroach, but only about 30 are considered pests. [#002] Cockroaches can eat just about anything, including glue, paper and soap. They can survive for long periods of time without any food at all. [#003] Insects and bugs can be useful in creating honey, wax, silk and other products. [#004] But they can also be killers, destroying some crops and carrying disease. [#005] When they are finished with their webs, spiders eat the silk to recycle it. [#006] Tarantulas can live for up to 30 years. [#007] Female nursery web spiders often eat the males. [#008] They do this after mating with them. [#009] Spiders have huge brains for their size. Some spiders' brains spill over into their legs. [#010] The crab spider can change colour to match its surroundings, to help catch its prey. [#011] The largest spider in the world is the Goliath birdeater tarantula with a leg span of 30 cm. [#012] The total weight of all the ants in the world is greater than the weight of all humans. [#013] There are more than 12000 species of ant. [#014] An ant can carry more than 50 times its body weight – the equivalent of a human lifting a small truck. [#015] Queen ants may live as long as 30 years. [#016] Only three types of animal fight battles in formation. They are humans, crows and ants. [#017] The Maricopa harvester ant is the most venomous insect in the world, with a sting equivalent to that of 12 honey bees. [#018] Worker, soldier and queen ants are all female. [#019] Male ants have just one job – to mate. [#020] In Thailand, weaver ants' eggs are eaten with salad. [#021] Termites first appeared on Earth around the same time as the dinosaurs. [#022] Soldier termites have such huge jaws they cannot feed themselves. They are fed by worker termites. [#023] Worker bees are sterile females that usually do not lay eggs. [#024] Bees dance to communicate with each other, often to explain where to find food. [#025] The honey bee stores the pollen it collects from flowers in pouches behind its legs. [#026] Honey bees visit between 50 and 100 flowers during one trip. [#027] A honey bee's wings beat about 11400 times per minute. This is what makes the buzzing sound. [#028] Africanized honey bees will chase you for 100 m if they feel threatened. [#029] Honey bees can only sting once, as their stingers get stuck in the victim's body. [#030] A queen bee can lay up to 200000 eggs per year. [#031] Only female wasps have stingers. [#032] Unlike bees, they can sting more than once. [#033] Some wasps sleep while hanging by their teeth. [#034] The most brightly coloured wasps are usually the ones with the most painful sting. [#035] There are more than 30000 species of wasp. [#036] Most species of wasp live alone, but about 1000 wasp species live in colonies. [#037] Scorpions can live in extreme conditions and some can even survive a night in a freezer. [#038] Some scorpions can

BRILLIANT beetles

About one-third of all animal species – more than 350000 – are beetles. [#091] Some female beetles may lay 1000 eggs in their lifetime. [#092] Beetles have poor eyesight, and communicate mostly using smells. [#093] Stag beetles take their name from their huge jaw, which looks like a stag's antlers. [#094] Beetles are found on every continent on Earth. [#095] The fringed ant beetle is the smallest known beetle. It grows to just 0.25 mm in length. [#096] The largest beetle is the Titan beetle at 17 cm long. [#097] The heaviest beetle is the Goliath beetle, which weighs 100 g. [#098] The Hercules beetle is really strong. It can carry 100 times its own body weight. [#099] Dung beetles feed on balls of poo. [#100]

slow their body down and survive on just one meal a year. #039 A female scorpion carries her young on her back until their skeletons harden. #040 There are nearly 2000 species of scorpion, of which 25 are deadly to humans. #041 Cat fleas prefer to live on cats but will live on humans if they have to. #042 The common cat flea can jump up to 200 times its own length. That's like you jumping over three football pitches. #043 Leeches are segmented worms that often live in water and suck the blood of other animals. #044 A leech has 32 brains. #045 A leech can eat up to five times its own body weight. #046 A mosquito's wings beat 500 times per second. #047 Before mating, male and female mosquitoes will synchronize their wing beats, so they are flying at the same speed. #048 Only female mosquitoes suck blood. #049 Mosquitoes have killed more humans than all the wars in history, because they spread the disease malaria. #050 Flies can smell meat up to 7 km away. #051 Houseflies can only eat liquids, but they turn many solid foods into liquids by spitting or vomiting on them. #052 Houseflies are particularly attracted to pet poo because it pongs and is easy for them to find. #053 Flies poo every four to five minutes. #054 Flies have poor eyesight, but they are good at detecting movement, which is why they are hard to swat. #055 Flies are the only insects to have two wings. Most insects have four. #056 When they take off, flies first jump up and backwards, before moving forwards. #057 A housefly's feet are 10 million times more sensitive than the human tongue to the taste of sugar. #058 Grasshoppers make music by rubbing their legs against their forewings. #059 Grasshoppers' ears are on the side of their body. #060 Locusts are grasshoppers that have come together in giant groups called swarms. #061 The largest swarm of locusts occurred in 1875 in the United States. #062 It was 3000 km long and 180 km wide. #063 Mantis have the largest claws of any insects. #064 The hooded mantis's body is shaped like two leaves so it can hide on plants. #065 Dragonflies can reach speeds of up to 50 km/h – faster than an Olympic sprinter. #066 A dragonfly's huge eyes give it almost 360-degree vision. #067 Parasitoid insects live inside other insects. #068 The smallest insect is the fairy fly. The males are just 0.14 mm long. #069 There are 92 different species of bedbug. #070 Bedbugs are blood-sucking insects that live in the cracks and crevices in and around our beds. #071 A caterpillar's first meal is the shell of its own egg. #072 Some caterpillars are brightly coloured as a warning to birds or other predators that they are poisonous to eat. #073 Caterpillars have just six legs. The rest of the legs you see are false legs. #074 Caterpillars spend all their time eating, increasing their body weight by up to 1000 times in just a few weeks. #075 Caterpillars may change colour as they grow. #076 Buff-tip caterpillars eat their way through leaves in teams. #077 Fly maggots feed on rotting flesh. #078 People who study insects are called entomologists. #079 Some types of cricket have ears on their legs. #080 A cricket's compound eyes enable it to see in many directions at once. #081 Earthworms' bodies are made up of segments. If a worm loses its back end, it can grow a new one. #082 An earthworm is a hermaphrodite, which means it is both male and female. #083 The largest worms live in hot countries and grow up to 3 m long. #084 Garden snails have over 14000 teeth on their tongues. #085 Snails move by squeezing and relaxing their muscles bit by bit, to make a rippling motion. #086 Slugs have four noses. #087 A slug's bottom is on the back of its head. #088 Slugs produce a constant trail of slime to stop them drying out and dying. #089 Most slugs eat plants, but some hunt down and eat other slugs by following their sticky trail. #090

8 foul facts about INVENTIONS

In the early 1900s, scientist **Marie Curie** discovered the radioactive elements **polonium** and **radium,** but she fell sick after carrying tubes containing the **dangerous** chemicals in her pockets. #001

In 1867, William Bullock developed **gangrene** and died after crushing his foot in **his own invention** – the rotary printing press. #002

The toilet snorkel was invented in 1982 to provide **clean air via the toilet bowl, in case of fire.** #003

In 1995, the babyvac

was invented to **clean snot out of babies' noses** so that they could breathe more easily. #004

26

In 2005, scientists in Singapore created a battery powered by

URINE.

#005

In 1908, George Hogan designed an alarm clock that **tipped water on to a sleeping person** to wake them up.

#006

The Aspire Assist Aspiration Therapy System was invented in 2013. It is a **weight-loss device** that pumps food out of your stomach before your body can digest it.

#007

Scientists in Japan have invented a **FART RECORDER** that **analyses a fart's smell** and then recreates it using a mixture of chemicals.

#008

12 facts about
SURGERY

ANCIENT ROMANS
practised plastic surgery to repair
noses, **eyes**, **lips** and **teeth**.
#001

One procedure in **ancient Rome** was
the removal of **scar tissue** from the
back, because it implied that a man had
turned his back in battle and was a
COWARD.
#002

Most surgeries in
Renaissance times
(14th–17th centuries)
were performed in
BARBER SHOPS.
#003

Many of the patients seen by
16th-century Italian surgeon
GASPARE TAGLIACOZZI
were treated for wounds caused by
DUELS or **STREET FIGHTS.**
#004

Tagliacozzi created **new
noses** using **ARM TISSUE.**
However, the new nose could
fall off if the person
blew it too hard.
#005

Australian artist Stelios Arcadious had an **EAR** grown from cells in a laboratory implanted in his arm to make him a living art exhibit. #006

About **17 million** plastic surgery operations are carried out every year worldwide… #007

…More take place in SWITZERLAND than any other country, with about **216 procedures** per **100,000 people** each year. #008

In the Middle Ages, surgeons used **herbs** and **alcohol** as simple anaesthetics. #009

The earliest form of surgery was **trepanning,** which involved cutting a small round hole in the head. #010

In 2007, a newspaper reported that a man in Colorado, USA, had his **THUMBS NARROWED** so that he could **use his iPhone more efficiently.** But the story turned out to be **fake**. #011

Some fashion-conscious women have a **toe bone removed** so that they can wear slim-flitting shoes. #012

9 facts about RUBBISH

Mumbai, India, gets rid of the horrid smell of its rubbish tip by pouring **thousands of litres of deodorant on it**. #001

The **Citarum River** in Indonesia is filled with the rubbish of **9 million people** plus the liquid waste of **500 factories**... #002

...In places, the water can no longer be seen beneath the moving carpet of rubbish... #003

...Boatmen still go on the river, but not to fish. **They look for things in the rubbish to sell**. #004

The Pacific is home to the **Great Pacific Rubbish Patch,** a vast soup of debris and chemical sludge that covers about **5000 km²**.
#005

About **6.3 billion kg of rubbish** is dumped into the oceans every year, **most of it plastic**. #006

When rubbish decomposes in a landfill, it produces methane gas – that's the smelly gas **in farts**. #007

In a landfill, cigarette butts take 12 years to biodegrade. **'Disposable' nappies take 800 years** to biodegrade. #008

Until the early 20th century, thrown-out food was mixed with **animal remains** to make a greasy gunk used in soaps and candles. #009

9 facts about POLLUTION

Linfen, China, is one of the most **polluted cities** on the planet due to the coal dust produced by the city's mines...

#001

In Ranipet, India, the **water in local rivers is SO TOXIC** that it **feels like an insect bite** when it touches the skin.

#003

...In fact, 16 of the world's 20 most polluted cities are in **China.**

#002

Over **1 BILLION** people in **the world** do not have access to **clean drinking water**, and **5000 people die** each day due to **dirty drinking water**.

#004

Some oceans have **dead zones** – nothing can live there because pollution has caused an **oxygen shortage**. #005

If you see COTTON BUDS on a beach, DON'T SWIM THERE. People flush them down the loo, so they're a sign that **untreated poo has flowed into the water**. #006

LONDON was once so THICKLY POLLUTED with coal smoke that it created a thick fog known as a **'pea souper'**. #007

Swimming and fishing are banned in Onondago Lake, New York State, USA, because it has so much **sewage and industrial waste**. #008

The **ACROPOLIS** is a collection of ruined buildings in Athens, Greece. Acid rain has caused these old buildings to **crumble** more **in the past 40 years** than they did in the previous 2500. #009

11 facts about SEWERS

In Victorian London, **HUMAN SEWAGE** drained into the River Thames, turning the **drinking water brown**.
#001

In Mexico City in 2000, heavy rain broke down the wall of a sewage canal. **Thousands of homes were flooded 1 m high with sewage**.
#002

In 1848, a law was passed in the UK stating that all houses should have an **ash pit, where poo and wee fell into a pile of ash** ready for collection.
#003

London built a modern sewer system after the **GREAT STINK OF 1858 WHEN A SMELL OF POO** hung over the city.
#004

Toilet paper was first used in **China** more than **1500 years ago**.
#005

34

Before toilet paper was widely available, rich people used **wool, lace** or **hemp** to wipe their bottoms, while the poor used **rags, leaves, sand or their hands**.

#006

The average person will go to the toilet about **2500** times a year and spend **3 years** on the loo in their lifetime!

#007

The toilet nearest the entrance in a public toilet is **likely to be the cleanest** because it is used least often.

#009

If you use a composting toilet, micro-organisms **break down the sewage into compost**.

#008

In New South Wales, Australia, so many **frogs invaded the public toilets** that the toilets stopped working.

#010

Rats are good underwater swimmers and can swim up pipes and **INTO YOUR TOILET.**

#011

11 GROSS FACTS ABOUT HOMES

Every time you flush the loo, **you send an invisible 2-m plume of bacteria** into the air that lands on exposed surfaces.

#001

The toilet is not the dirtiest place in the bathroom,

IT'S THE SINK. The sink has **20,000 germs** per square centimetre, but the toilet seat only has **20 germs per square centimetre.** #002

Locals in Florida, USA, found that **Cuban tree frogs** had swum up their pipes into their toilet bowls. #003

A kitchen chopping board has **200 per cent** more bacteria than the average **toilet seat**. #004

Brown rat droppings are like mouse poo, but

three times larger. #006

Mouse droppings are easy to identify because they are **6 mm long, black** and **shaped like grains of rice**. #007

Black rat droppings are more **sausage-shaped,** and look like fatter jelly beans. #008

Bat droppings look like mouse droppings but are **shiny, speckled** and **always found in a pile**. #009

COCKROACH POO

looks like small dark specks. #011

Bird poo contains **acid,** which eats into house bricks and damages them. #010

12 facts about Crazy Royals

English King Henry VIII had a **Groom of the Stool** – a man who **wiped his bottom** for him. #001

English King Henry II had a jester called Roland the Farter, who would **fart on demand**. #002

To keep guests entertained at a feast, Roman emperor Caligula would **behead** criminals in between courses. #003

When his sister died, Caligula was so upset **he banned people from laughing, on pain of DEATH**. He also banned them from taking a bath. #004

Louis XIV of France only took **three baths** in his lifetime. #005

In 1762, Korean Prince Sado was **locked in a rice chest** by his father. He died after eight days. #006

King Nabonidus of Babylon thought he was a **goat,** and insisted on **grazing in a field**. #007

Duke Gian Gastone of Tuscany **stayed in a stinking bed for 7 years,** refusing to get up. #008

By the time he died, aged 55, Henry VIII was **covered in boils** and so **overweight** that he couldn't move about by himself. #009

Don Carlos, son of Spanish King Phillip II, forced a shoemaker to **eat a pair of shoes** that weren't up to standard. #010

Anna of Russia built an **ICE PALACE** to celebrate the marriage of a prince she did not like. She made the married couple stay there on their wedding night. #011

When they had finished building St Basil's Cathedral in Moscow, Russian Tsar Ivan the Terrible had the designers **blinded,** so they could never build anything better. #012

13 CANNIBAL
FACTS

One of the Aztecs' favourite recipes was a **human stew** called **'tlacatlaolli'**. #001

In the Middle Ages, some people ground up **ancient Egyptian mummies** to make medicine. #002

Aztec priests ritually sacrificed enemies, **ripping their hearts out** and **eating their bodies**. #003

Hot human blood, distilled brains and **powdered human heart** have all been used as possible cures for epilepsy. #004

The Korowai tribe on south-east Papua were cannibals **up until the 1970s,** when they met outsiders for the first time. #005

'Mellified man' medicine, made from **soaking a human corpse in honey,** was used in Arabia in the 1100s. #006

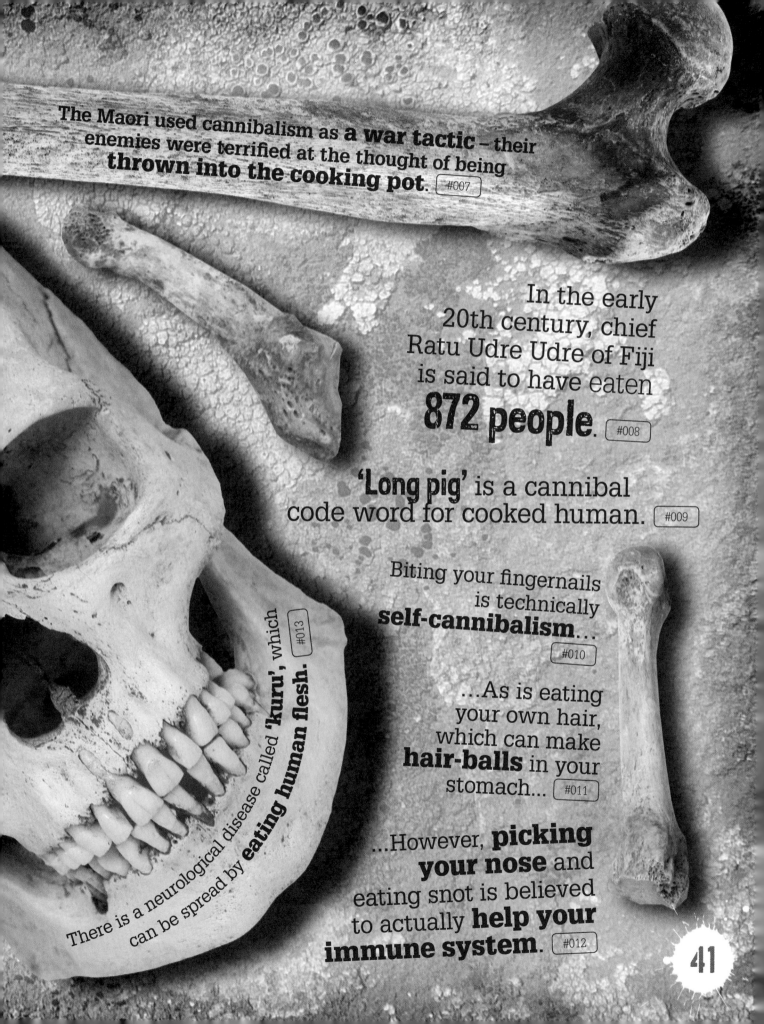

The Maori used cannibalism as **a war tactic** – their enemies were terrified at the thought of being **thrown into the cooking pot**. #007

In the early 20th century, chief Ratu Udre Udre of Fiji is said to have eaten **872 people**. #008

'Long pig' is a cannibal code word for cooked human. #009

Biting your fingernails is technically **self-cannibalism**... #010

...As is eating your own hair, which can make **hair-balls** in your stomach... #011

...However, **picking your nose** and eating snot is believed to actually **help your immune system**. #012

There is a neurological disease called 'kuru', which can be spread by **eating human flesh.** #013

41

11 Perilous Pirate facts

The worst pirates were **hanged**, and their bodies were **covered in tar** and left to **rot publicly** in an iron cage. #001

After **William Kidd** was caught in 1701, his corpse was left to rot for **three years**. #002

Pirates would collect fresh food when they landed, but on ship it quickly went **stale or mouldy**. Not eating enough good food often made pirates sick – their **teeth fell out** and their **skin went pale**. #003

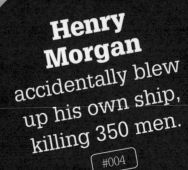

Henry Morgan accidentally blew up his own ship, killing 350 men. #004

Edward Teach was also known as **Blackbeard**. When he attacked a ship, he'd tie lit

gunpowder

fuses into his beard to scare his victims. #005

Edward Teach liked to drink **rum** mixed with **gunpowder**. #006

Pirate flags were designed to **terrify people**, sending the message **'surrender quickly or die'**. #007

MINOR OFFENCES

were punished by flogging pirates with a knotted rope. #008

As punishment, a pirate might be dragged on a rope under the ship... #009

... **He would either drown** or be slashed by the razor-sharp barnacles on the ship's hull. #010

A cheating fellow pirate would be left on a desert island with little food or water, and a **loaded pistol** to kill himself #011

9 facts about
EGYPTIAN MUMMIES

It took 70 days for the ancient Egyptians to make a mummy out of a dead body. #001

First, they cut open the body with a **sharp stone**, then removed the **stomach, lungs and other organs**, and put them in jars near the body. #002

The HEART was left inside the body. It was thought to be vital for the AFTERLIFE. #003

A sacred **scarab beetle** was placed on the heart. #004

Using a hammer and chisel, they knocked a **hole** into the nose bone and hooked out the **brain**. #005

The Egyptians thought the brain was unimportant, and threw it away. #006

Then they stuffed the body with **bandages** and **sawdust**, covered it completely with salt and left it for a month to dry out. #007

After the month, they wrapped the mummy in RESIN-SOAKED BANDAGES while casting spells over it. #008

Pharaoh Tutankhamun's mummy shows that he may have **died from gangrene** (a stinking flesh-rotting infection) after he broke his leg. #009

INDEX

ACKNOWLEDGEMENTS

t = top, b = bottom, l = left, r = right, c = centre

Cover images courtesy of istockphoto.com and Shutterstock.com
4l Dragon_fang/Dreamstime.com, 5r Nruboc/Dreamstime.com, 6tl
sdominick/istockphoto.com, 8tr Shell114/Shutterstock.com, 8cl
princessdloft/istockphoto.com, 9tl Eleonora Kolomiyets/Shutterstock.
com, 9br gorilla images/Shutterstock.com, 10–11 Shutterstock.com,
11tr tehcheesiang/Shutterstock.com, 12l Dreamstime.com, 13bl Bevan
Goldswain/Shutterstock.com, 15bl kati1313/Dreamstime.com, 19tc
Jubal Harshaw/Shutterstock.com, 20–21 istockphoto.com, 20tc Paul
Fleet/Dreamstime.com, 20bc Peter Waters/Shutterstock.com, 21tc
Xenobug/Dreamstime.com, 21c ex0rzist/Dreamstime.com, 22tl
Darrenp/Shutterstock.com, 23tc istockphoto.com, 27t koya979/
Shutterstock.com, 27cl Chaoss/Dreamstime.com, 29tc okili77/
Shutterstock.com, 29bl Stuart Jenner/Shutterstock.com, 30–31
Dreamstime.com, 32 hxdbzxy/Shutterstock.com, 33 Dragana
Gerasimoski/Shutterstock.com, 36bl SteveBower/Shutterstock.com,
38b Maksym Bonderchuk/Shutterstock.com, 39bl Elenathewise/
Dreamstime.com, 40–41 all Shutterstock.com, 44–45 pzAxe/
Shutterstock.com, 44c Cosmin Manci/Shutterstock.com.